How To Write Your First Business Plan

With Outline and Templates Book

By

Boomy Tokan

Content

The Comprehensive Business Plan Template 6

The Five Parts of a Business Plan 6

Part 1: The Marketing Plan: "What I Want To Do" 8

Industry overview – Past, Present & Future 8

Sector overview: – Past, Present & Future 9

Competitors: 9

Product/Service: 12

Testing: 13

Place: 14

Price: 16

Marketing/Promotions: 18

Customers: 19

Business Name: 22

Part 2: The Operations Plan: "How I Am Going To Do It" 24

Management: 24

Business Structure: 25

Sole Trader/Self Employed (Unlimited Liability) 26

Partnerships (Unlimited Liability) 27

Limited Company (Limited by Liabilities) 27

Company Limited by Guarantee 28

USA BUSINESS STRUCTURES: 29

Limited Liability Company (LLC) 30

Partnerships 31

Corporation..31

Staff:...32

Insurances:..33

Training Requirements:..34

Exhibitions:..34

Part 3: The Financial Plan: "What It Will Cost To Do It" ...35

Cash flow Forecast: 35

What does a Cash flow Forecast look like? 35

Columns:..36

Picture 2 38

Rows:...38

Picture 4 42

Profit and loss account: 42

Part 4: Appendices: "Additional Supportive Information"
....46

Letters of intent:...46

Letters of recommendation:...46

CV:..47

Other Literature:...47

Part 5: The Executive Summary 48

Here are the parts to write about under the "Summary"

or "Executive Summary"......................................48

The Power Point Business Plan Template 50

A little bit more about the PPBP...50

Slide Seven: "Income/Financial Potential" 56

Other Books by Boomy Tokan..62

Boomy Tokan – Profile 64

FREE Bonus
"How To Start Your Own Business In 30 Days"

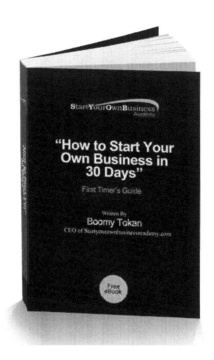

Hey ... If you would like to learn how to start and run a "High Performance" business; then download this FREE guide. It will also show you how to start making money from your business within 30 Days!

"How To Start Your Own Business In 30 Days"

Copy and paste in your browser:

www.startyourownbusinessacademy.com/freedownload1

Enjoy

The Comprehensive Business Plan Template

Generally speaking, most comprehensive business plans have the same information in them. They may have been given other titles but the basic format and requirements are the same. Hence the template I am giving you may not be the exact format you may have received from your local business adviser or accountant but the information within it will be the same. Also the format I am giving you has been tried and tested and I have personally used it to raise thousands for many of my clients.

The Five Parts of a Business Plan

Think about your hand. It has five fingers, right (hopefully)? Or just imagine you have five fingers. In the same way I want you to know that there are five parts to a business plan:

1. The Summary; also called "Executive Summary" or "Introduction"

2. The Marketing Plan

3. Operations Plan

4. Financial Plan

5. Appendices

These are the names I have used and it is easy for me to remember them. If at the end of the book you feel you want to call them something else then feel free to do so. The only proviso is that if you are trying to reach other people with the plan, they need to be familiar with or understand the terms you give the plan.

What Does Each Name Stand For:

1. **The Marketing Plan** – "What I Want To Do" - What type of business are you wanting to start? What market do you want to start your business in? Who do you want to cater to?

2. **The Operation Plan** – "How I Am Going To Do It" – What kind of business structure do I need for this enterprise? Who do I need to network with? Do I need a mentor?

3. **The Financial Plan** – "What It Will Cost To Do It" - What are the costs of production, cost of sales or monthly expenses? How much profit will the business make in 12 months?

4. **Appendices** – "Additional Supportive Information" - like letters of intent, letters of recommendations, CV etc

5. **The final part which is the first one or two pages of your plan is the "Summary" or "Executive Summary".** Which is the summary of all the above 4 (Marketing Plan, Operations Plan, Financial Plan and Appendices). The general advice given is that this section must be written last and I agree to that. You will understand more as we build up the business plan.

Once you understand this then you are ready to progress to the next stage.

Part 1: The Marketing Plan: "What I Want To Do"

The marketing plan, when not researched correctly, has far reaching consequences:

1. If the marketing plan is wrong, then every other part of the business plan will be wrong. i.e. if you create a product that people do not want, then the way you plan to structure the business (Operations) and what you think it will cost (Financial) will be wrong.

2. If the information you have about who your customers are is wrong then the business will not work.

3. If the information you have about your competitors are wrong then the business will struggle.

4. If the way you have defined your market is wrong then the whole business will collapse like a wobbly stool!

Trust me when I say the Marketing Plan is the most important part of the business plan.

So, What Is Included In The Marketing Plan?

Industry overview – Past, Present & Future

a. Let's say you want to start a business selling baby food. Your Industry overview is the information you can find out that relates to the overall food industry. Information such as: what has happened in the past to food consumption, how much does the average household spend on food and what are the projections for the consumption of food? How many babies are born in your area; nationally or internationally? (Don't worry this information is readily available online and at your Business Libraries; start there.)

b. Industry Overview is important because it exposes you to vital trends that may affect your business. Some businesses are so seasonal that this information can make or break the business.

Sector overview: – Past, Present & Future

a. Using the same Baby food sales business example: Baby Food is a sector within the Food Industry so this business will need to know how much food babies consumed in the past, what they are consuming now and what they are likely to be consuming in the future. You might want to know an estimate of how many children are born per year and what the projections are for the following 10-20 years.

b. Remember most businesses never consider the future. They are too busy trying to deal with the day to day aspect that they are not planning for the future. Do not acquire this mind-set. Writing your business plan offers you the opportunity to think and plan ahead and position your business greater than what your competitors do!

Competitors:

You can bury your head in the sand and convince yourself

wrongly that there are no competitors for your business or you can take an active approach to learn from your competitors and use the information to further your business.

Competitors come in 3 shapes and sizes:

a. Direct,

b. Indirect

c. Future Competitors

Let's break this down: If you are a Hairdresser located on a high street your Direct Competitor are other established Hairdressers in your vicinity 1-2 miles radius. Your Indirect Competitors could be those Mobile Hairdressers or those working from home or even those located 5-10 miles away that your potential customers can drive to. Your Future Competitors are those in schools and colleges studying Hairdressing.

Therefore investigating your competitors has become extremely important. The kind of information you want to know about your competitors include and not exclusively:

a. S.W.O.T. – What are their Strengths, Weaknesses, Opportunities and Threats?

b. Manufacturers – Who are they working with?

c. Relationships – What kind of business relationships do they have?

d. Finance – How are they financed? By shares, loans or personal funds?

e. Suppliers – Who supplies their products? (Hang around outside their shop or business)

f. Consumers – What kind of customers do they have? – age, sex, etc.

g. Promotion Strategy – How do they promote themselves? (Visit their website and read local papers as well.)

h. Geographical Coverage – How far do they operate?

i. Product Range – How many types of products do they sell or do they offer other attractive services?

j. Culture – What is their work culture?

k. Staff – How many? What ages? Sex? Etc.

l. Size – How big or small is this business in terms of sales or profits?

m. Cost Structure – How do they charge?

n. Reputation – What do people say about them both good and bad

o. Ownership - Who owns the business? Is it a franchise?

p. Distributors Used – Who are they?

q. Segment Served – Do they cater to a particular niche?

r. Motivators Beyond Money- Can you find out?

s. Management – Who manages the business? Do they have a Dragon giving them advice?

t.   Industry Opinion – What do experts say about them?!

You might need to do some hard detective work but you are only able to develop your products/service once you know what others are doing. Otherwise you will set up a business that will just be like the rest; struggling businesses!

Where Do You Get This Information?

a.   Visit Local Stores

b.   Shared Customers

c.   Shared Accountants

d.   Lawyers/Solicitors

e.   Suppliers

f.   Reports Exhibitions

g.   Internet

h.   Local Business Libraries

i.   Industry Magazines

Companieshouse.gov.uk (if they are a limited company they need to log their annual accounts here. You can down load it and find useful information about your competitor's Sales, Finance, Staff, Loans etc all for £1-£3

Product/Service:

Now that you have done the above research you are ahead of most people who have an untested idea and force it on the market only to discover someone else next door has the exact product/service and he is struggling.

Since you know what your competitors are doing, which has given you insight into the market, you know what the experts are saying about your industry and what/how your niche (sector) is doing. You are ready to create a Unique Product/Service.

Even if you have been working in an industry for years and you believe you will be the next Steve Jobs, research is still vital to your success.

Remember that your product must be solving a problem. People do not simply pay for a product; they pay for what the product can do for them! Invariable thinking like this will help you identify your target market when you consider "who has the problems I can solve?"

Ask yourself these questions about your product/service:

a. Does it meet expectation of customers?

b. What advantage will it have over competitors' products?

c. What is unique about your product/service?

d. Why should customers buy your products/service?

e. What is it made of?

f. How is it made?

g. What Benefits does it have?

Testing:

Ensure you have a method of testing and collating useful data that helps you make decisions on your products/services. As Eric Ries from "Lean Start-up" says; it is better to release a Minimum Viable Product (MVP) rather than trying to create a perfect product in isolation.

What this means is that you should conduct numerous experiments that you can learn from. Don't wait until you have a completely ready product before you get your potential customers involved in the research/sales process.

Years ago I learnt that marketing starts in the product development stage as opposed to after you have completed what is deemed to be the best product for your target group.

So to recap:

- Get a focused group or some of your potential clients

- Conduct market test with your product/service

- Document the feedback and make changes to your product/service

In this section of your business plan you can document the results that back up your claim that you have a winning product/service!

Place:

Although a place can be a physical location, the place can also be a Social Media Platform. If you have a Graphic Design Business the place does not have to be a high street or physical location it can be a Facebook Page or a Website! The important point to consider is "where can my clients and potential clients best find me?" Resist the temptation to rush out and hire an office as many are in the habit of doing.

Ask yourself these questions:

a. Can I work from home?

b. Can I hire a meeting room when I need it?

c. Can I meet at McDonald's or Starbucks?

d. Can I meet at the clients' office?

e. Can I share an office?

f. Can I really afford an office?

g. What would my clients appreciate?

h. Are my clients concerned about an office?

If you do consider having a physical office as the best options for your business then find one that satisfies the following:

a. Affordable

b. Accessible

c. Good transport links -Tube lines Buses & Trains

d. Proximity to potential customers

e. Any other advantages

Let the reader know why you have chosen your location. You must at this point include the advantages and disadvantages of the location you have chosen.

Price:

Let me be upfront by saying that competing on price as your major competitive driver can be suicidal to your business. I hear new businesses say this all the time. If asked how they will compete as a new business the first thing they say is that they will charge less than the competition.

Remember what I said earlier: your product of service must be solving a problem". The question is: what is the value of that solution to your customers?

For example, those who do plastic surgery are expected to charge a good price. If a new person appears on the scene and start charging 70% less than the average price, only a fool will use the service!

Let's use the same monetary example for Beauticians business. Those women who are used to paying £40 for a set of nails would run from you if you started charging £20 because they will perceive you do not know what you are doing!

So your price must be competitive but not low enough to attract the wrong perception of your business. Be aware that a business that always gives a quality service will be much more appreciated than one who charges below market rate for a 2nd rate product/service.

So How Should You Price Your Products/Services

  a. Total Cost plus profit: This means that you add the costs that pertain to each unit of sale and add a profit on top; that will be your selling price. One of the problems you must watch for is your initial cost may be so high

b. that you could overprice yourself out of the market! Make sure this pricing structure is used in consideration of what competitors charge.

c. You could also discover that your total cost is less. Therefore you are able to charge below market rate for your products. Our computer ink supplier has a shop in a local estate and therefore able to keep the price of ink at almost 30% below market price simply because his actual cost are so low!

d. Competitors Price: How much are your competitors charging. If the competitors are charging say £100 for a unit of product you might choose to charge the same. You might even charge £120 and deliver the best possible service to that niche therefore picking up the top end clients who are always looking for something extra in terms of service.

e. Ability for customers to pay: In some markets what the customers are prepared to pay may just be the guiding principle on how much to charge. This is very typical of the antique business where the customer really determines the market rate. If you are operating in this type of market then the way you determine your price will be different.

f. Standard & Average Price: Again, looking into the market to determine what the average prices are can help you select the best price for the product/service.

Whatever price point you choose be sure that it makes you money and covers your costs; otherwise you will not stay in business long. So write about your pricing strategy here!

Marketing/Promotions:

Remember that your aim is Niche Marketing. Here is a definition that will help you: Niche Marketing is defined by www.businessdictionary.com as concentrating all marketing efforts on a small but specific and well defined segment of the population. Niches do not 'exist' but are 'created' by identifying needs, wants, and requirements that are being addressed poorly or not at all by other firms, and developing and delivering goods or services to satisfy them. As a strategy, niche marketing is aimed at being a big fish in a small pond instead of being a small fish in a big pond.

Promoting is an aspect of marketing. When we think about marketing we ought to be considering how we plan to make potential clients interested in what we are offering. When we offer a discount to the client we are promoting the product/service.

Whatever the strategy, it must be:

a. Cost effective: Can you afford this strategy?

b. Measurable: Do you know how many people it brought into the buying funnel? For example, spending money on a 1 page ad in a paper may not be measurable unless you place a coupon that must be downloaded and you can measure the expense by the number of downloads.

c. Reach the right people: Am I reaching the right target group with this advert?

d. Generate sales: As a result of this exercise, did I make more money?

e. Penetrate markets: Did this strategy open me up into new markets in which I was not known?

f. Manageable: Was I able to manage the new level of business generated?

The first place to begin your campaign should be online. It is easy to test products online, try out an idea or even measure your success there.

No matter what strategy you choose as a new business you need to be working on:

a. Getting traffic

b. Forming Relationships

c. Converting these relationships into people who buy your products

d. This simple system can transform your business if done properly

So what is your marketing strategy? What do you plan to do to promote your products?

Customers:

If you want to hear ridiculous business rhetoric ask some new business owners who their potential customers are; you will hear answers like "all the women over the age of 25 that live in the UK" or "Everyone that watches films". These type of answers are more broad than the length of Route 66 in the

USA. Even brands like Coke cannot boast of such a broad customer base; how much more a small business.

Let's play up to our strengths and start thinking about a "Niche". I love this definition of what a Niche Market is ....a very small segment of individuals who share a narrow set of wants, needs and wishes

www.csbrand.com/Brand_Glossary.ihtml

This is the key to success of Small Businesses. Your job is to keep on finding and keeping customers that fit into this group!

So let us see how we might define who our customers are. I once asked a Christian Gospel Artist who her potential fans would be; I like the answer she gave which fits into a niche. She said, "My fans are aged from 30-55. They buy both CD albums and downloads of Urban Gospel Music. They are generally professionals or business owners who love quality singing delivered in an Urban Music style. They do not follow fads (like auto tuned music) and go out to events perhaps 4 times a year and would pay £10-£20 easily. They are tech savvy and mostly use Facebook and Smart phones!"

This type of knowledge identifies specifics that will make marketing efforts easier. It is not broad like saying "everyone that listens to Urban music" or "every Christian". It tells us their age, work type, social media activities, etc. The artist knows that ads on Facebook are a must, sending texts will work and live events must be part of the strategy.

So now what about you? Have you identified your customers? If in doubt, why not start by looking into your competitors' customers? Also what type of people generally like your products/service? What needs does your product/service meet? Who needs it the most and are willing to pay for it?

This is a list of areas to research:

a. Past Needs

b. Present Needs

c. Future Needs

d. Who They Are

e. Where They Are

f. What Do They Buy

g. In What Quantities

h. How Often Do They Buy

i. Age Group

j. Education

k. Social media platforms they use

l. How Will I Market To Them

m. Why Are They Buying From The Competitor Now

n. Income

o. Profession

p. Favourite DJ

q. Radio Station

r. TV Program

 s. Social media platform

I am sure you can think of more questions!

Business Name:

I am going to make a statement here that many people will probably just ignore but I will make it anyway because I know that by the time they realise the authenticity of it they will come back and read this section again. The statement is that – You should not choose a name you like but one that works for your business!

Choosing a name today is a tad more complex than it was a few years ago when local competition was limited due to size of an area or number of people. What I mean by that is 50 years ago a local bakery can be called Dave's Shop and everyone will know it because the community was small enough to even know the owners children and their dog. If you try that today you will be in for a nasty business shock!

What you should consider before you choose a name:

 a. Does the name communicate what the business does? Dave's Bakery is miles better than Dave's shop.

 b. Is there anyone else using the same name?

 c. Can I get a .com or any other domains for this name?

 d. Can the name be registered at the Company's house or any other business agency?

 e. Can the name readily translate to an image?

 f. Does it solve a problem potential customers may have

It should only be when the above have been carefully considered do we choose a name.

One final point is that start-up businesses must always look to niche their products. A name that communicates well with potentially customers will always gain more online traffic, be more attractive and eventually make more money than the one that is too broad!

Part 2: The Operations Plan: "How I Am Going To Do It"

In this section of the business plan I am going to give you 6 areas you need to pay attention to. Operations plan is a crucial part of the plan not only because I say so but because this section contributes tremendously to all the other parts of the plan. Without a well thought-out Operations Plan you could throw your well-formed marketing plan into the mud as some do!

Here we go:

Management:

For the purposes of the business plan, management refers to those that will advise you or be involved in the daily running of the business. Especially if this is the first business you are running; you need a team. Even if you have run many businesses you should know the importance of a team. What you need to ask is "Who can help me?" There are 4 areas of help:

a. If you live in the UK every local government has Business Development Advisers working for the borough. This is generally free and they can advice you for a long time. Find similar organisations in your country.

b. Experienced business persons; even if they are within a different industry. Most business needs are the same. The differences are in the niche. This type of person will still be a great help in guiding you in the right way; a good sounding board.

c.   Join a Business Club. This could be a great idea as well since it attracts like mined people.

d.   Business opportunists. Those looking to provide advice for share of ownership or for a fee at the time of existence in 2-5 years. These people might come in the form of Business Angels!

When thinking about this it is worth mentioning that you will need to determine what they are capable of contributing into your business. Ask yourself: What have they achieved? What business are they in? Are our gifts complementary?

In your business plan, write about whom they are and the effects their contribution will make.

Business Structure:

So ask yourself: "What is the best structure for me?"

The answer depends on (amongst others):

a.   Level of potential liability

b.   Potential 1st year income

c.   How funding will be raised

d.   Potential tax liabilities

e.   Potential profit in the 1st year

f.   Business experience

g. Type of business – Profit or Non for Profit

If you can be stung with a heavy liability if anything goes wrong then you must set up a limited company even if you do not have the experience to administer one. The reason is that it is one of the few structures that provide liability protection.

If the amount of income in the first year is less that £30k and the expenses will also be low then a Sole Trader structure will be most ideal (broadly speaking).

If you want to raise investment funding then a Limited Company will be of interest to the investors because it allows them to own shares in the business. If your business is delivering services with a social end in mind and you want to access grants quickly then a Company Limited by Guarantee is the best option. (This applies to the UK. See USA business structures below)

So you see the structure really depends on you and your business. Getting good advice as suggested in the first point in this chapter is key.

Let's look at the advantages of the 4 most common types of business structures:

Sole Trader/Self Employed (Unlimited Liability)

Advantages:

a. No need for registration

b. Inexpensive

c. No need for audit

   d. Lower NIC (£2.50 per week)

   e. Tax paid later, losses can offset against future profits.

Disadvantages:

   a. Personally liable for all debts

   b. May not sound professional

   c. Can be difficult to get credit

   d. Expansion plans curtailed by what one person can

Partnerships (Unlimited Liability)

Advantages:

   a. Same as the sole trader

   b. The ability to spread risks, because there are 2 or more persons

Disadvantages:

   a. Personally liable for all debts

   b. The need to draw up partnership agreements

   c. Could fall out with partners

Limited Company (Limited by Liabilities)

Advantages

   a. Limited liability

   b. Separate legal entity (Can employ the best

man/woman for the job)

c.   May sound more professional

d.   Perpetual succession

e.   Increased borrowing power

Disadvantages:

a.   Can cost up to £200 to incorporate

b.   Audit required if turnover exceeds £1m

c.   Annual accounts to be submitted annually

d.   Loss of privacy – Ex:- drawings, etc

e.   Annual meetings of members are compulsory and must be minute.

f.   Tax losses cannot be offset against personal losses

Company Limited by Guarantee

Advantages

a.   Provides opportunities to get grants and other government funding

b.   Limited liability

c.   Separate legal entity (Can employ the best man/woman for the job)

d.   Protects services benefactors because the business is run by Trustees

Disadvantages:

    a. Loss of control

    b. No share ownership

    c. No dividends payable all money's is ploughed back in

    d. Non-profit structure

Once you have decided on the type of structure you will implement then you should write your reasons for your choice and the advantages and disadvantages of the choice made!

USA BUSINESS STRUCTURES:

Sole Proprietorships:

Like the Sole Trader in the UK, the Sole Proprietorships is a very easy to establish business structure. Most one man business in the USA operates under this structure. Whilst you can still employ others, the day to day running of the business plus the ultimate responsibilities and liabilities lay with the one person in charge of the business.

Advantages

    a. Quick to establish
    b. In many states may not require license
    c. Decision making process can be quick – no bureaucracy
    d. Can pay taxes as you go along and balance paid at year end

Disadvantages

    a. Unlimited liability

    b. Can limit access to funding

    c. The notion of "two is better than one" is not at work in this case

Limited Liability Company (LLC)

Business owners who want protection and maintain flexibility choose this type of business structure. Whilst it is not a requirement by law, members of an LLC should create agreements that will detail how profits will be shared, working hours, responsibilities etc. Invariably this ensures the smooth running of the business. All LLC must file articles with the secretary of state and the cost can be as small as $40 or an average of $200. It is imperative to seek further advice and information from state websites for the full registration requirements. Advantages

    a. Limited liability

    b. Can be attractive for funding

    c. Can be structured to suit the owners

    d. Can incur a reduced tax liability via "Pass through" – Allowing taxation to the person and not the business

Disadvantages

    a. Taxation can become complex if people live in other states

b. Cost of hiring a lawyer (It is not required but beneficial)

Partnerships

Sometimes a number of people may come together to carry on a business/trade, where this occurs it is considered a partnership. Irrelevant of the enthusiasm that exists in the beginning, those entering into this business structure should get a Partnership Agreement drafted by a lawyer or developed and signed by all the partners. States have their own legislations that deal with the requirements of Partnerships. The IRC Title 26 has details of codes relating to partnerships. Advantages

a. People working together

b. Pool of people contributing money for common goals

c. The pool of skills available

d. The support system it provides

Disadvantage

a. You could be jointly and severely liable for debts

b. Working with others can be complex

c. Decision making can also become more difficult than sole trader at this stage due to the variety of opinions

Corporation

This is a separate legal entity owned by shareholders. The

Corporation itself is liable for taxes, losses not the shareholders. Businesses are subject to federal and state taxes.

Advantages

a. Can raise money from outside sources

b. Offers a robust legal structure

c. Good liability protection

d. Can issue shares and bonds

Disadvantages

a. Strong formalities to adhere to

b. Requires annual tax, report filing

c. Can only be operated by experiences owners

Staff:

Questions that have always baffled people in relation to staff are: When do I begin hiring? How much staff should I hire? How much do I pay? are some of those questions. Here are guiding principles:

- Have a contract worker instead of an employee. An employee is on your payroll but a person on contract submits an invoice to you. An employee has to get paid every week/month whether the business makes money or not. A contracted worker can only get paid for the work done.

- For as long as possible until your business is financially strong, use a contract worker.

- Hire the staff you can afford. Do not feel obligated to get someone you cannot afford.

- Get as much help from family and friends. Call on favours.

- Only start hiring when your business is in a financial position to do so!

Insurances:

Did you know that not all insurances are compulsory for a business? Let's go through some of them.

Compulsory:

a. Employers' liability insurance

b. Motor insurance

Non Compulsory:

a. Professional indemnity

b. Fire and special perils

c. Loss of money

d. Loss of earning

e. Goods in transit

f. Public liability

g. Product liability

h. Legal expenses

Here is the advice: though some are not compulsory it is sensible and wise to have an insurance cover for an eventuality. If you are running a business that sells products which are hazardous, then you should have Public Liability or Legal Expenses insurance. Otherwise a claim can ruin your business!

Training Requirements:

In this section you can write about the training you would like to gain. List the institutions that offer them, express when you would like to go on the programme, also outline the costs and make sure you carry this into your financials. Write also how you feel the training will help the growth, establishment and profitability of your business.

Exhibitions:

Going to exhibitions can cost a lot of money but can be very useful in attracting new business, making niche contacts, getting your name out and general networking.

Exhibitions should be used in 2 ways:

a. Just the cost of the gate fee can produce tremendous amount of contacts if you network well.

b. Taking out a stand: Taking out a stand can cost you a great deal of money and you must be sure you have the staff and administrative know how to cope with an influx of enquiries if that happens.

Part 3: The Financial Plan: "What It Will Cost To Do It"

This section is one to be taking very seriously because Cash is King. There is the saying, "Look after the pennies and the pounds will look after themselves."

Every cost or expense you plan to make over a given period must be put into the cash flow forecast so that a correct financial picture can be generated. We need to consider 2 tools in this section:

a. Cash flow forecast

b. Profit and loss account

Cash flow Forecast:

Is a document that shows the In and Out of cash within a business on a (mostly) monthly basis over a given period of an estimated 12 months. The cash flow forecast can be quite sobering and brings to bear the financial realities of a business. However you need to make sure the figure you put in are as realistic as possible.

What does a Cash flow Forecast look like?

It is divided into

a. Columns and

b. Rows

Columns:

A Cash flow Forecast has at least 14 columns (Top to Bottom).

The first columns are for items (names of where the money or expenses come from). The next 12 with be for each of the months of the year and the last one is for totals. See Pictures 1 & 2

Picture 1

	A	B	
1	Cash Flow Forecast	Pre Start	
2		PERIOD	
3			
4	Receipts		
5	Cash Sales		
6	Invoice Payments		
7	Capital Introduced		
8	Loans Received		
9			
10	Other		
11	Income		
12	**Total Receipts**	0	
13			
14	Payments		
15	Cash Purchases		
16	Payments to Creditors		
17	Employee Wages & National Insurance		
18	Own Drawings/National Insurance		
19	Motor/Travel Expenses		
20	Rent & Rates		
21	Postage & Packing		
22	Advertising & Printing		
23	Heat, Light, & Power		
24	Telephone		
25	Professional Fees		
26	Insurance		
27	Repairs & Renewals		
28	Bank Charges & Interest		
29	General Expenses		
30	Loan Repayments (Bank)		
31	Loan Repayment (Other)		
32	VAT Payments		

Cash Flow / P & L /

Picture 2

	A	B	C	D	E
1	Cash Flow Forecast	Pre Start			
2		PERIOD	Month1	Month2	Month3
3					
4	Receipts				
5	Cash Sales				

K	L	M	N	O
Month9	Month10	Month11	Month12	TOTAL
				0

Rows:

A Cash flow Forecast has in excess of 15 rows (Left to Right).

    a. The first row tells us of the names of the months

    b. Next the rows that are the items making up the income section

    c. Then the items followed by the totals of the income section

    d. Then the rows listing the expenses that pertain to each month and then the totals for the expenses.

    e. Then we have the differences between the expenses

and income less the previous balance. A new balance is produced carried over to the next month and the process is repeated the next month until the end of the period.

See Pictures 3 & 4

For further assistance send me an email to: **boomytokanauthor@gmail.com** and I will send you the Template that can do your Cash flow calculations as well as the Profit and loss accounts free.

Picture 3

	A	B	C	D	E
1	Cash Flow Forecast	Pre Start			
2		PERIOD	Month1	Month2	Month3
11					
12	**Total Receipts**	0	0	0	0
13					
14	**Payments**				
15	Cash Purchases				
16	Payments to Creditors				
17	Employee Wages & National Insurance				
18	Own Drawings/National Insurance				
19	Motor/Travel Expenses				
20	Rent & Rates				
21	Postage & Packing				
22	Advertising & Printing				
23	Heat, Light, & Power				
24	Telephone				
25	Professional Fees				
26	Insurance				
27	Repairs & Renewals				
28	Bank Charges & Interest				
29	General Expenses				
30	Loan Repayments (Bank)				
31	Loan Repayment (Other)				
32	VAT Payments				
33	Capital Purchases				
34	Other				
35					
36	**Total Payments**	0	0	0	0
37					
38	Cashflow Surplus/Deficit (-)	0	0	0	0
39	Opening Bank Balance	0	0	0	0
40	Closing Bank Balance	0	0	0	0

	F	G	H	I	J	K	L	M	N	O
	Month4	Month5	Month6	Month7	Month8	Month9	Month10	Month11	Month12	TOTAL
	0	0	0	0	0	0	0	0	0	0
										0
										0
										0
										0
										0
										0
										0
										0
										0
										0
										0
										0
										0
										0
										0
										0
										0
										0
	0	0	0	0	0	0	0	0	0	0
	0	0	0	0	0	0	0	0	0	0
	0	0	0	0	0	0	0	0	0	
	0	0	0	0	0	0	0	0	0	

Picture 4

31	Loan Repayment (Other)						
32	VAT Payments						
33	Capital Purchases						
34	Other						
35							
36	Total Payments	0	0	0	0	0	0
37							
38	Cashflow Surplus/Deficit (-)	0	0	0	0	0	0
39	Opening Bank Balance	0	0	0	0	0	0
40	Closing Bank Balance	0	0	0	0	0	0
41							

								0
								0
								0
								0
0	0	0	0	0	0	0	0	0
0	0	0	0	0	0	0	0	0
0	0	0	0	0	0	0	0	
0	0	0	0	0	0	0	0	

Profit and loss account:

I like this definition from investorwords.com for a Profit & Loss Account: An official quarterly or annual financial document published by a public company, showing earnings, expenses, and net profit. Net income is determined from this financial report by subtracting total expenses from total revenue.

The profit and loss statement and the balance sheet are the two major financial reports that every public company publishes. The difference between this statement and the balance sheet deals with the periods of time that each one represents. The profit and loss statement shows transactions over a given period of time (usually quarterly or annually), whereas the balance sheet gives a snapshot of holdings on a specific date; also called income statement or earnings report.

This document looks at your annual sales loss, the expenses and calculates the profit for the year. Although, only some of the figures in the cash flow are used, the profit and loss account gives a clearer profitability figure. See Picture 5

For further assistance send me an email to: boomytokanauthor@gmail.com and I will send you the Template that can do your Cash flow calculations as well as the Profit and loss accounts free.

Picture 5		
Profit & Loss		
RECEIPTS		
Sale		0
Other Income		0
A.	TOTAL INCOME	0
Direct Costs of		
Production/Sale		
Purchases		0
Staff Costs		
B. TOTAL DIRECT		
COSTS		0
c.	GROSS	
PROFIT (A-B)		0
OVERHEADS		
Salaries/Wages PAYE, NI		0
Rent/Rates		0
Light/Heat/Power		0

Insurances		0
Repairs/Maintenance		0
Promotion/Advertising/Printing		0
Travel/Motor		0
Telephone		0
Postage & Packing		0
Professional Fees		0
Proprietor's Drawings		0
General Expenses		0
Bank Charges		0
Loan Interest		0
Depreciation @ 20%		0
Misc.		0
D.	TOTAL	
OVERHEADS		0
NET PROFIT/LOSS		
(C-D)		0

Part 4: Appendices: "Additional Supportive Information"

4 types of literature should be in this section:

  a. Letters of intent

  b. Letter of recommendation

  c. Your CV

  d. Other literature that support the plan

Letters of intent:

These letters are written by potential or existing customers that will buy the products/service or use more of it once you get started.

Letters of intent can be strong persuasive tools when seeking to raise money. What they communicate is that you will get sales when you get going. Banks and other funders love letters of intent. Your job is to get between 2-20 letters of intent that can be attached to your business plan.

Letters of recommendation:

These are also similar to letters of intent although they do not express any commitment to buy from you but they communicate valuable support. Your job is to get between 2-20 letters of recommendation that can be attached to your business plan.

CV:

Whatever you decide to put in the CV make sure you communicate your business and expertise knowledge as it relates to the business.

Other Literature:

Statistics, Pictures or any other document can be placed in this section.

Part 5: The Executive Summary

The final part of your business plan which consists of the first one, two or three pages of your plan.

As I said earlier the Summary or Executive Summary should be the last part of the plan to be written. Unless you are a seasoned business plan writer you would need to stick to this rule.

One very important point to mention is that most people who would read your business plan will read these one, two or three pages first and then decide whether they are interested in further reading. This means you should spend a good amount of time ensuring the plan sustains the reader's interest!

Here are the parts to write about under the "Summary" or "Executive Summary"

a. **Background:** This is where you talk about your experience in business and other work related expertise. This information can be taken from your Appendices.

b. **Market:** Briefly detail the products or services you are offering as well as the market potential for them. You can discuss the opportunity as you see it and how you plan to capture the given market segment. This information can be found in your Marketing Plan.

c. **Business Challenges** and how I plan to overcome them: One of the most adventurous concepts floating amongst some seasoned business people is that you should be upfront about the challenges your business will face. At the onset many shy away because they may feel exposed. Saying the challenges upfront (and the methods you would use to overcome them) puts you in a position of strength and gives the impression that your plan has been well conceived and will be well executed. This information can be found in your Marketing Plan, Operations Plan and Financial Plan.

d. **Profitability:** Here, you should discuss the figures taken from your Profit and Loss account and Cash flow Forecast and mention how profitable your venture is likely to be.

e. **How much do you need:** Answer the big question here! This figure can also be obtained from your Cash flow Forecast.

f. **Finally:** Read and reread your content. Make sure there are no errors. Check and cross check your figures and make sure they are correct too. Also make sure your plan is well laid out. Do all these and follow the above information so that you have a better chance of writing a good Business Plan.

The Power Point Business Plan Template

In this section I am going to teach you how to write a simple Business Plan in

Power Point. Although I've known about this for a long time, I usually only teach it in my Management Courses. However, I taught a group of Start Up businesses recently and when I mentioned this type of Business Plan they all seemed to love it. As a matter of fact I went home and used the template I am about to give you to write a plan for one of my businesses.

The PPBP (Power Point Business Plan) is useful for a number of reasons:

1. It is much more simple and easy to write.

2. It gets you started. It can be just the start needed to write the complete plan detailed above.

3. Since you can add pictures/videos, the plan can be extremely aesthetic.

4. Acts as a useful presentation to funders

5. Can be written in 1 – 3 hours or one day max(assuming you have the info)

6. It is a great way to learn how to present because this allows you to practice with friends & family.

7. Absolutely anyone can write one!

A little bit more about the PPBP.

It requires a maximum of 12 slides and a maximum of 7 bullet points on each slide. (Can I suggest you use only about 10 slides and add additional slides if it is absolutely essential. Part of the attraction of this PPBP is that people can understand you quickly without the need for lengthy information)

Do remember that one of the reasons you are using this medium is the opportunity to talk people through the slides so keep your bullet points short and to the point, leaving you room to speak. It may also be useful if it gives just enough information so that someone reading it may understand without your physical presence. Finally in regards to presentation add your logo to every page and use picture where needed

So let's begin:

Slide One: You guessed right Yes! The Cover Page.

This should contain the following information:

a. Your Business name

b. Your name

c. Words like "Summary Business Plan" 20__ to 20__

d. Your logo

Slide Two: Guessed yet? Ok it's "Business Background". Use this slide to write the following information in bullet points:

a. Type of businesses you have run before

b. Where you have worked and job title. This is important especially for those who are just starting in business and therefore do not have any business experience. Your work experience demonstrates seriousness and product/service knowledge.

c. Any business background/experience your team possess could be good as well.

d. If you have delivered any training you can also mention it here.

e. Previous products developed can be mentioned on this slide as well.

In one of my business plans, these are three of the bullet points I wrote:

a. Worked as a Business Adviser and Trainer at Portobello Business Centre

b. Worked as a Lecturer at City University.

c. Set up and ran businesses in Fashion, Property, Music and Retail

Slide Three: "What You Have Achieved So Far" This is where you really need to start selling yourself:

a. List all the successes you have had. Even if you have never run a business before you can talk about successes you have had on a job or project.

b. Talk about achievements no matter how small they may seem.

c. You might even include the comments people have made about you.

d. If you have reached certain personal or work targets this is the place to talk about it.

e. Business failures can be mentioned if turned into learning experiences

Writing something that will inspire; confidence is essential

In one of my business plans these are three of the bullet points I wrote:

a. Everyone who has attended attests to the quality and relevance of the workshop

b. Workshop is delivered below budget

c. Received 2 invitations from other agencies that want us to deliver the workshop

Slide Four: "The Opportunities As You See It" This slide essentially discusses why you are getting involved in this type of business. You should mention the following

a. Opportunities that exist in the market

b. The types of products you believe people want

c. Mention whether the market is favourable for new entrants

d. If you have an innovation that can provide a cutting edge within the niche

e. Ideally you should use S.W.O.T. (Strengths,

Weaknesses, Opportunities, and Threats) to analysis one of your competitors.

In one of my business plans these are three of the bullet points I wrote:

a. Deliver FREE webinars to attract online audiences to gain traffic

b. Deliver courses for existing businesses in Newham and London wide

c. Build a successful brand

Slide Five: "The Team" For some of us this could be the very first time we have to think about having a team. I am writing this section right after delivering a business Start-up Course. At that course everyone seems to look blank when I spoke about their team. Who? Your Team. Yes your Team! So who should be part of your team?

a. A business mentor

b. Those who complement you

c. Another shareholder or partner perhaps

d. A marketing person if that is not your strength

e. An administrative person if that is not your strength

f. Any individual that is capable of adding value to your business should be part of your team.

In one of my business plans these are three of the bullet points I wrote:

a. We have a Facebook expert

b. In house experience Business Adviser

c. 2 experienced course administrators

Slide Six: "Your Business Model"

Let me start by giving you two definitions of what a business model is:

"It is the plan implemented by a company to generate revenue and make a profit from its operations. The model includes the components and functions of the business, as well as the revenues it can generate and the expenses it could incur"

Another definition is:

"A Business Model is the particular way in which a business organization ensures that it generates income; one that includes the choice of offerings, strategies etc".

From these two definitions we observe that every business including a Start-up like yours should be contemplating on how it plans to use its available resources in a strategic way to make money.

This is the slide that provides you with the opportunity to express how you have planned to make money.

In one of the business plans these are three of the bullet points I wrote:

a. Use the Facebook platform to attract fans and convert them into paying clients

b. Create and run 24 cost effective courses per year

c. Work with existing agencies within a 5 mile radius

Slide Seven: "Income/Financial Potential"

Not only for the sake of investors but it is for your sake to detail the amount of money you hope to earn from your business activities. For example if you are delivering 3 products/services it is important that you write down how many of each item you hope to sell over a given period; say a year.

A clearly defined financial objective will help you work out what your potential income could be. Rather than say your business will make 100k in the first year, this slide should help you define exactly hope you plan to do this, the number of items you plan to sell and the total expenditure that will facilitate that income

In one of my business plans these are three of the bullet points I wrote:

a. We could run at least 24 paid courses per year with at least 10 people earning an average of £6,000 - 12,000

b. Sale of course material 200 - 500 units at £30 each = £6,000 - £15,000

c. Expenses are set as 30% of all income generated

Slid Eight: "How Much Do You Need"

a. You must be able to detail this figure. One useful

strategy that will help you determine how much you need for your business is to think about the cost of delivering the product/service as well as the cost per item. After that you can add on the general expenses like telephone or heating bills that do vary with output parse.

b. Take the example of a company delivering training programs. The set up cost could be £1000 which can be made up of the price of a laptop, projector, room hire and Facebook page setup.

c. If they plan to deliver one training per month and room hire will be £200 per training, plus £200 per program for marketing budget the amount of money they need can be £1000 + £4800 (£200 x 12 for room hire for the year & £200 x 12 for 12 months marketing spend for the year) = £5800 + (Other expenses like phone, heating and so on.)

This type of company can actually run the business on the initial £1000 since people will pay to come to the course before it happens plus you do not need to spend on a course until it is due to happen. Other businesses will vary!

So you need to determine how much you need.

In one of my business plans these are three of the bullet points I wrote: Start-up cost (Not the cost for the whole year)

a. £200 for Facebook setup

b. £200 to create course material and books

c. £150 for screen recording software

Slide Nine: "When You Will Pay Back – Exit Strategy/Repayment"

Anyone giving you money in form of a loan or investment will want to know when they are getting their money back. This is very normal. When you can pay back the entire amount borrowed will largely depend upon the profitability position of the business.

    a. The best thing is not to offer repayment in such a way that jeopardises the business' future or restrict business growth. Although business loans from banks will generally prefer a monthly payment, make sure you negotiate a realistic repayment amount and period.

    b. Give a conservative payment period and do not give a timescale you might struggle to meet. Better to "understate and over deliver" than to "overstate and under deliver!"

In one of my business plans these are three of the bullet points I wrote:

    a. Repay £100 every month

    b. Full payment by the next 12 months

Slide Ten: "Contact Details"

This is the last and final slide and you should place in the slide with all of your most up-to-date contact and information so that some can get back to you if necessary.

What should be on this slide?

a. Name and Surname

b. Email address

c. Telephone number

d. Facebook page - url

e. Website address – url

f. Twitter address

g. Blog address

GOD Bless and Happy writing!

Thank you so much for reading my book. I hope you really liked it.

As you probably know, many people look at the reviews on Amazon before they decide to purchase a book. If you liked the book, **could you please take a minute** to leave a review with your feedback?

You can do that right here.

www.amazon.com/Write-Your-First-Business-ebook/dp/B009T8XHBS/ref=cm_cr_pr_pb_i

60 seconds is all I'm asking for, and it would mean the world to me.

Thank you so much,

Boomy Tokan,

T: +44 7932 394620

E:boomy@startyourownbusinessacademy.com
W: startyourownbusinessacademy.com #: @boomybizbooks

FREE Bonus
"How To Start Your Own Business In 30 Days"

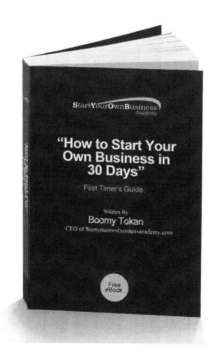

Hey ... If you would like to learn how to start and run a "High Performance" business; then download this FREE guide. It will also show you how to start making money from your business within 30 Days!

"How To Start Your Own Business In 30 Days"

Copy and paste in your browser:

www.startyourownbusinessacademy.com/freedownload1

Enjoy

Other Books by Boomy Tokan

Book Title: How To Raise Money For Your Business: The Ultimate Guide For Start Up Businesses; Book

If you want to know the truth about raising money for your business this book is for you. If you are having a tough time raising the money you want for your business this book is for you too. If you are not sure where to go to get the kind of funding you need for your business this book is just what you need.

After many years of helping businesses of various kinds raise the money they want, I have laid out in print all that you need to know about raising money for your start-up business!

New Year's Resolutions: The Guide to Getting It Right Why

Many New Year Resolutions Fail Within 30 Days How To Make Yours Work and Kick Start Your Year Book. (The Right Guide)

As the year unfolds, many people like you will be making resolutions they want to achieve over the next 12 months or for the coming years. Most may never succeed without the right techniques. Let this book cut down your learning time by teaching you a few principles that will ensure your New Year's Resolutions succeed!

The Bad Girls Of The Bible – 7 Most Infamous

Ever wondered why some people are just – bad? In this book you will discover some well-known characters and other obscure ones that can teach you life lessons for the 21st Century. This book will educate and inspire you!

Boomy Tokan – Profile

Boomy Tokan is the founder and business tutor of **"Start Your Business in 30 Days" programme.** His experience spans across practical involvement in business and training of more than 1000 Start Up Business owners.

He has set up and run businesses in Property, Music, Management, and Fashion industries. **Many were very successful and others failed miserably.** Through them all he has learnt tremendous lessons that make him a knowledgeable, instructive and experienced teacher!

Whilst at Portobello Business Centre in London (One of the leading Enterprise Centres in Europe), **Boomy Tokan created and delivered Business** Training Programs plus One to One advice to Start Up Business. He has also taught "The Business Planning" programme at City University London.

Over the past years **he has helped raise more than £300,000 (nearly $500,000) in small amounts for small businesses.** His experience on writing business plans and his understanding of how to raise finance has been of great benefit for many people.

As a Business Seminar Speaker he continues to contribute to the lives of many people. Those who attend his courses say: *"This facilitator knows what he is about and has a wide field of experience" Charles A "I realise that I can just get up and do it...." Ros S "Very insightful and encouraging" Precious O "Great workshop" Peter D "This workshop was very helpful" Lillian J* and many more!

Boomy believes in giving back to the community and so he runs courses for Newham Business Start Up in London where he helps the underprivileged to access life transforming business information.

He has written over 100 articles for ezine.com and is a author of 3 books ("How to Write Your First *Business Plan*: With Outline and Templates Book"; "New Year's Resolutions: The Guide to Getting It Right"; "How to Raise Money for Your Business: The Ultimate Guide For Start Up Businesses"**)** published on Amazon Kindle that have entered the top 100 of the Entrepreneurship and motivational categories. His books are simply loaded with useful information that is life changing.

His book on "How To Write Your First Business Plan" has received over twenty four 5 Star reviews with comments like:

"This is really a comprehensive guide to writing a business plan." **Sandra**

"The book reads very easily, and the examples provided allow for a quick understanding of what the author is writingabout." **Luke Glasscock**

"It was detailed while still maintaining a comprehensible overview of the structure and what should be taken into account when writing your business plan." **Michael Matthews**

Have You Got Your FREE "Start Your Own Business In 30 Days" Guide

Made in the USA
Lexington, KY
08 March 2014